DATE DUE			
FE 27 '06			
OC 09 '06			
APR 2 2 '08			
NOV 1 6 '10			

20TH CENTURY MEDIA

MEDIA

70s & 80s

GLOBAL TECHNOLOGY

Please visit our web site at: www.garethstevens.com
For a free color catalog describing Gareth Stevens Publishing's
list of high-quality books and multimedia programs, call
1-800-542-2595 (USA) or 1-800-387-3178 (Canada).
Gareth Stevens Publishing's fax: (414) 332-3567.

Library of Congress Cataloging-in-Publication Data

Parker, Steve.
    20th century media / by Steve Parker.
        v. cm.
    Includes bibliographical references and index.
    Contents: [1] 1900–20: print to pictures. [2] 20s & 30s: entertainment for all.
  [3] 40s & 50s: power and persuasion. [4] 1960s: the Satellite Age. [5] 70s & 80s:
  global technology. [6] 1990s: electronic media.
    ISBN 0-8368-3182-9 (v. 1: lib. bdg.) — ISBN 0-8368-3183-7 (v. 2: lib. bdg.) —
  ISBN 0-8368-3184-5 (v. 3: lib. bdg.) — ISBN 0-8368-3185-3 (v. 4: lib. bdg.) —
  ISBN 0-8368-3186-1 (v. 5: lib. bdg.) — ISBN 0-8368-3187-X (v. 6: lib. bdg.)
    1. Mass media—History—20th century—Juvenile literature. [1. Mass
  media—History—20th century.] I. Title: Twentieth century media. II. Title.
  P91.2.P37   2002
  302.23'09'04—dc21   2002022556

This North American edition first published in 2002 by
Gareth Stevens Publishing
A World Almanac Education Group Company
330 West Olive Street, Suite 100
Milwaukee, Wisconsin 53212 USA

Original edition © 2002 by David West Children's Books. First published in Great Britain
in 2002 by Heinemann Library, Halley Court, Jordan Hill, Oxford OX2 8EJ, a division of Reed
Educational and Professional Publishing Limited. This U.S. edition © 2002 by Gareth Stevens, Inc.
Additional end matter © 2002 by Gareth Stevens, Inc.

Designer: Rob Shone
Editor: James Pickering
Picture Research: Carrie Haines

Gareth Stevens Editor: Dorothy L. Gibbs

Photo Credits:
Abbreviations: (t) top, (m) middle, (b) bottom, (l) left, (r) right

BFI Stills, Posters and Designs: page 13(m). Bridgeman Art Library: page 24(tr). BSkyB: page 17(bl).
Corbis Stock Market: cover (m, bl), pages 8(bl), 25(ml). The Culture Archive: pages 17(mr), 23(tl), 27(b).
Intel Corporation (U.K.) Ltd: page 19(bl). ITN: page 13(tl, tr).
JVC: cover (br).
The Kobal Collection: pages 13(br), 22(t), 23(bl).
Mirror Syndication International: page 13(mr). Charley Murphy (computer graphics), Hames Williams
  (photography), and Leonardo da Vinci (painting), cover for Utne Reader, 34, July/August 1989: page 25(tr).
Popperfoto: pages 4(tr), 11(tl), 12(both), 15(bl), 18(t), 26(t), 27(m); Reuters: pages 3, 5(bl), 6(both),
  8(tr), 9(r, bl), 10(t), 14(tr), 16(tl), 17(tl), 24(b), 26(b).
Redferns/Richie Aaron: page 20(tr); Tom Hanley: page 20(bl); Paul Massey: page 19(m);
  Ebet Roberts: page 21(m). Rex Features: page 7(m).
Science Photo Library/Ed Young: page 9(t). Sony: page 11(br). Frank Spooner Pictures: page 21(br).
Topham Picturepoint: pages 7(tl), 10(b), 23(r), 27(t), 28(b).
Vin Mag Archive Ltd.: pages 4(br), 5(br), 7(br), 18(b), 19(t), 21(tr), 22(b), 28(tl, tr), 29(br).

Printed in the United States of America

1 2 3 4 5 6 7 8 9 06 05 04 03 02

20THCENTURY MEDIA
70s & 80s
GLOBAL TECHNOLOGY

Steve Parker

Gareth Stevens Publishing
A WORLD ALMANAC EDUCATION GROUP COMPANY

CONTENTS

The early 1980s saw the first mass-produced personal computers. By the end of the decade, they were five times smaller, twenty times more powerful, and could be linked into media telecommunication networks.

The "blockbuster" movie tradition started in the 1970s with the monster box-office hit Jaws (1975). Anyone who had ever gone swimming in the ocean, or even in the bathtub, could relate to the fear in this film.

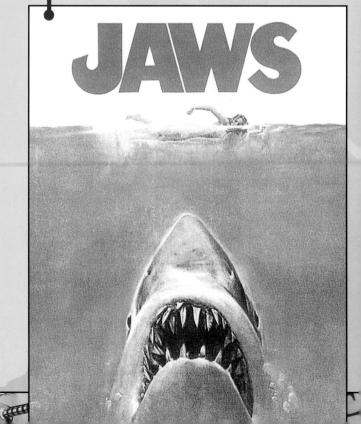

MORE FROM THE MEDIA

In 1970, the main forms of news media were newspapers, radio, and television. These mass media also provided opinions and commentary, features, and entertainment. In more specialized ways, books and magazines offered the same kinds of communication. The main forms of entertainment media were films, records and tapes, works of art, and photographs.

By 1990, the list of media had changed very little, but choice and convenience had greatly increased. More radio stations and television channels, from space and through cables, were on the air — day and night! Viewers could record their TV shows on videotape, to play later. The compact disc, at first a new format for recorded sound, became a computer storage device offering "multimedia" at your fingertips.

For economy, speed, and fun, graphic designers loosened the distinctions between whole words and their abbreviations, initials, and images.

Opening the Berlin Wall in East Germany was a major media event in 1989. It signaled the collapse of communist systems in Eastern Europe, raising hopes for democracy, freedom, and peace.

The Simpsons *began its world conquest on December 17, 1989. This prime-time family cartoon comedy helped blur the division between adult and children's TV.*

SPECIAL REPORT

Newsweek
THE INTERNATIONAL NEWSMAGAZINE

The Wall
1961-1989

FAMINE!

A terrible famine in the mid-1980s devastated the lives of people in the African country of Ethiopia. Watching scenes of the starvation, disease, slow death, hopelessness, and appalling suffering, TV viewers around the world cried openly. Magazine and newspaper photos and radio reports direct from the area caused similar emotions.

HUMAN TRAGEDY

The reasons for this profound human tragedy were many and complex. In this dry, barren region, farming had always been difficult. Years of attempting intensive agriculture had taken what little goodness there was and turned the soil to windblown dust. Then, this region of normally sparse rainfall had drought for several years. Amid political unrest, regional groups fighting for control plundered the country's economy to buy weapons, rather than food and medicine.

This mother and child were two famine victims in a relief camp for 5,000.

Dozens of aid centers, like this one in Korem Wollo province, were set up to care for the thousands of Ethiopians with no shelter or sanitation and precious little food, water, and medical care.

Live Aid came from the USA and the UK at the same time.

1.5 BILLION VIEWERS

Popular music was one of the first media to campaign for famine relief. In late 1984, Britain's star-studded Band Aid recording, "Do They Know It's Christmas?," raised awareness of the Ethiopian plight, as well as millions of dollars for relief efforts. USA for Africa did the same with "We Are the World." Band Aid's mastermind, rock musician Bob Geldof, next organized the Live Aid concerts on July 13, 1985. Live Aid was a transatlantic fund-raising extravaganza featuring performers from both old and new popular music, linked by a global media system of satellites and TV and radio networks.

EPIC SUFFERING

By 1984, the tragedy had reached epic proportions. Huge relief camps were filled with weak, ill, and starving people who had lost everything except a few ragged clothes. Journalists and television crews came to report news stories, but even hardened reporters were so moved by the scale of the disaster that their voices shook with emotion as they described the situation.

Journalists at the scene were often overcome by the horrible sights, sounds, and smells of the Ethiopian relief camps.

7

For months during 1984 and 1985, the situation in Ethiopia dominated headlines and reports in almost every medium.

THE WORLD WAKES UP

Images of skeleton-thin, swollen-bellied babies, born innocently into a nightmare of pain and deprivation, were especially powerful. The world began to take notice, and the media played a leading role. Campaigns started to generate response from rich nations, especially the industrialized West. Celebrities from music, movies, television, literature, and other media spearheaded appeals for aid — short-term food, medicine, tents, and equipment and long-term programs to help the people eventually be able to help themselves.

RAJIV'S INDIA
Can He Make It Work?

Newsweek
THE INTERNATIONAL NEWSMAGAZINE
June 3, 1985

We Are The Children
The New Wave of Sympathy and Aid May Come Too Late to Save Africa's Lost Generation

CABLE AND DISH

Broadcasted from transmitters and tall towers, coded radio signals, traveling at the speed of light, carry the pictures and sounds for television. The signals are picked up by receiver aerials on houses and other buildings. At least, that's how it was in 1970.

LINKS IN SPACE

Since the 1960s, satellites had been used to relay TV signals across continents and oceans, but the links were focused, narrow beams between the very large, dish-shaped transmitters and receivers of TV companies. Then, the signals were fed to ground-based transmitter towers for broadcasting to the general public. The 1980s brought a new system — Direct Broadcast Satellite (DBS).

Many technologies link on-the-spot news teams with general networks. In 1981, this transmitter dish sent TV pictures of Prince Charles and Lady Diana's wedding from St. Paul's Cathedral in London.

8

SATELLITE TV

DBS is what most people now call "satellite television." The broadcaster sends signals up to a satellite, and the satellite beams the signals down over a wide area, called the "footprint." The signals are powerful enough for small receiver dishes to detect, so anyone with suitable equipment can get them. Japan began regular DBS transmissions in 1985. In Europe, the Astra satellite started sending out Sky TV programs in 1988.

Broadcasters send and receive signals for TV and radio via satellites, using huge dishes. TV operators can receive specially coded signals from a satellite TV company, decode them, and distribute them through their cable networks.

CABLE TV

The United States developed cable TV, in 1949, to provide better television reception in remote regions, such as mountain areas, that were hard to reach with ground-based signals. Operators such as CNN (Cable News Network), MTV (Music Television), and ESPN (Entertainment Sports Programming Network) gradually joined with ground and satellite systems and major networks to share and retransmit.

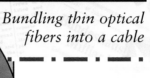

Bundling thin optical fibers into a cable

A growing concern in the 1980s was that DBS dishes, especially on beautiful and historic buildings, were ruining the view, so new rules were introduced to govern their locations.

Fiber-optic cables could carry not only TV, but also radio, computer links, phone calls, and on-demand music and movies.

LASER LIGHT TV

Another route for television signals is in the form of coded pulses of laser light, flashing along bundles of hair-thin glass rods called fiber-optic cables. These cables are usually laid underground and must be connected to every home individually. The United States led the cable revolution with more than 8,000 cable companies connected to some 50 million homes by 1990.

During the 1970s and 1980s, the outsides of buildings belonging to the big TV networks were adorned with dishes, all of them pointing at satellites.

9

SO MANY CHANNELS

In the 1980s, TV technologies leaped ahead, and the pathways that delivered television to homes multiplied. What would the extra hours of airtime on all these new channels bring? More news, game shows, and light entertainment, of course, but many channels also saw opportunities for new content.

INDEPENDENT SUCCESSES

New programming included experimental products, particularly offbeat comedies and dramas. Some failed. Others became cult viewing, especially among younger people. Often, these programs were first made by small, independent production companies, while major networks played it safe with their established audiences. If a new show made it big, however, the networks lined up to buy broadcasting rights.

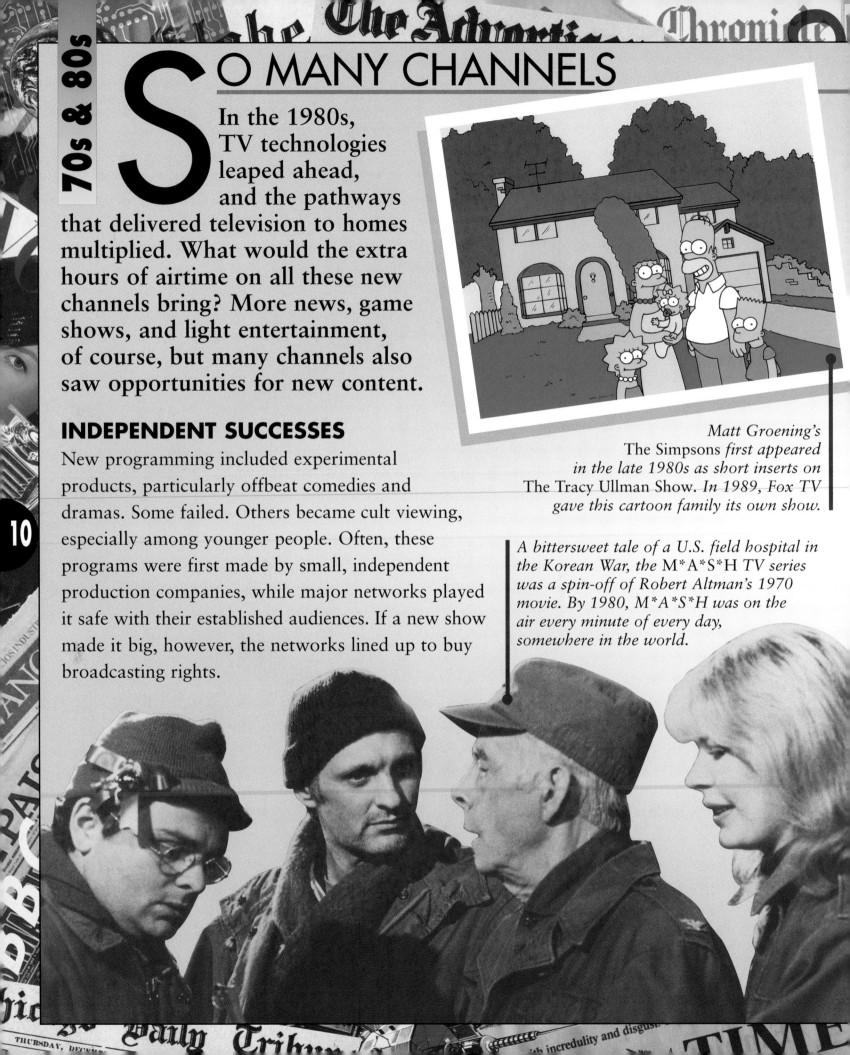

Matt Groening's The Simpsons *first appeared in the late 1980s as short inserts on* The Tracy Ullman Show. *In 1989, Fox TV gave this cartoon family its own show.*

A bittersweet tale of a U.S. field hospital in the Korean War, the M*A*S*H *TV series was a spin-off of Robert Altman's 1970 movie. By 1980, M*A*S*H was on the air every minute of every day, somewhere in the world.*

Monty Python's Flying Circus *was first shown in the United Kingdom (1969–1974). Its zany, anarchic humor poked fun at its own medium with forgotten lines and false endings.*

SPECIALIZED CHANNELS

Extra TV airtime also led to more specialized channels. Some were dedicated to a single area of interest, such as the Discovery Channel, others to a particular target audience, such as the Children's Channel. The Cartoon Channel was just for fun, while the Shopping Channel was just for spending money.

RECORDING TV

A new gadget that people in the 1970s could buy was a videocassette recorder, or VCR. Magnetic videotape was already being used in TV studios to record programs for later transmission. Home versions allowed people to change their viewing habits by recording programs, while they were doing something else, to watch later. At first, the TV and movie industries protested against home video recorders, but then they cashed in by selling films on video. Television was becoming more flexible, more convenient, and all-encompassing.

FEATURE FILMS ON DISC

Around 1978, several disc-based formats were developed to show movies and other longer types of films on a TV set. Based on compact disc (CD) technology for sound recording, they provided quality superior to home videotapes. Most TV watchers, however, were not anxious to buy the systems, partly because they only played and did not record.

At first, movies on discs drew limited interest.

Video recorders were first advertised as time-shift devices, but movie and TV companies believed they would be used for illegal copying. Many court battles followed.

Early formats for home video were Sony's Betamax and JVC/Matsushita's Video Home System (VHS). Longer recording time, the economy of mass production, and support from the huge RCA company led VHS to victory.

INSTANT NEWS

"We interrupt this broadcast to bring you a news flash. A gunman has fired shots at the president of the United States, Ronald Reagan. Details are still coming in."

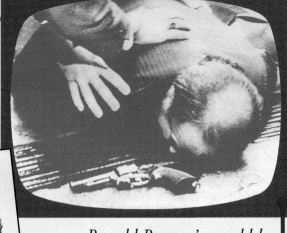

Ronald Reagan's would-be assassin, John Hinckley, was quickly subdued.

When President Reagan was shot, on March 30, 1981, near the Hilton Hotel in Washington, D.C., some of his bodyguards risked their own lives to shield him, while others overpowered and disarmed his attacker.

IN SECONDS

Television crews and news photographers at the scene of the attempted assassination of Ronald Reagan recorded the event. TV channels always monitor each other's news, so as soon as one channel broke the story, others joined in within seconds. In moments, pictures and reports of the shooting were flashed around the globe by radio, cable, and satellite. The possible death of the world's most powerful man was so important that announcers broke into scheduled TV and radio programs.

TELETEXT

A system called teletext, that could broadcast words and graphics along with TV signals, was introduced in the 1970s. Sent out with normal TV programs, the teletext signals took up only a tiny part of the broadcast. They were displayed, instead of the usual images, on a properly equipped TV set, and the viewer could select the content.

Weather information by teletext

A *news bulletin requires great effort from a network's staff, including writers, producers, and videotape editors. As a bulletin starts, reports are still coming in and must be put together.*

AS IT HAPPENS

Although television cameras became small enough for one person to carry, feeding live pictures and sounds into telecommunication networks, rather than recording them inside the camera to play back later, was a problem. The problem was resolved in the 1980s with a cable or short-distance transmitter link from the camera to a nearby vehicle that had a large dish on it for a direct satellite link. Because every second counts, both on the scene and in the studio, working in the news media is stressful. The effects of this stress have been explored in several movies.

STILL GOING STRONG

Radio was far less costly to produce than TV, so, to compete, it could afford to be more localized and specialized. Just a few hundred listeners might be enough to attract the advertising to pay the bills. By the mid-1980s, the United States had 9,000 radio stations, which was 1,500 more than ten years earlier.

The world's media gathered at a press conference given by Manchester United soccer star George Best (seated, left) and the team's manager, Matt Busby.

13

In the 1976 movie Network, *news anchorman Howard Beale has a mental breakdown and threatens on-air suicide.*

In the film The China Syndrome *(1979), a TV news reporter helps find out the truth in a cover-up of a nuclear power plant accident.*

THE SHINY DISC

The compact disc, or CD, is now a familiar format for storing music and other sound recordings, as well as computer games, programs, files, photos, and many other forms of information, or data. Back in 1982, the CD was very new, and some people doubted it would succeed.

ANOTHER FORMAT?

During the 1970s, many large electronics and media companies experimented with digital technology, in which information is coded as on-off signals, or bits, rather than the continuous up-and-down waves of analog technology. Computers work digitally, and digital recordings could provide much better quality, so digits were seen as a step forward. Sound recording media, however, already included vinyl disks, or records, and various forms of magnetic tape, even convenient cassettes. Was there room for another format?

EARLY DOUBTS

Japan's Sony Corporation said "yes." By 1982, supported by Philips of the Netherlands, CBS, and the Polygram Corporation, Sony had produced the first CD players. The public, however, was not enthusiastic. The sound quality was better, and you could conveniently skip to any part of the recording almost instantly, but would music-lovers forsake their stereos, tape players, and huge record collections?

The microscopic pits that carry the on-off digital codes give CDs a rainbowlike gleam. The surface is protected by a layer of ultraclear plastic.

WHY THAT SIZE?

For a long time, Akio Morita (1921–1999), Sony's founder, had wanted a convenient, durable, digital method of storing sound. Norio Ohga, who succeeded Morita as chairman of Sony and was trained in music, advised that a 75-minute recording would be long enough for almost any piece of classical music. This amount of time set the CD's size at 4.7 inches (12 centimeters) across.

Akio Morita was "Mr. Sony."

SUCCESS!

In November 1984, Sony marketed the D-50, a small, portable CD player, hoping it would become as popular as the Walkman, Sony's portable radio and audiocassette player, and revive the CD market. It did. The D-50 was quickly nicknamed the Discman. In just another year, the number of different musical recordings on CDs shot past 10,000. The CD format was here to stay.

CBS/Sony produced the first fifty CD titles, led by Billy Joel's *52nd Street* and including classical, pop, and rock styles. One of the biggest early successes was *Brothers in Arms* (1985) by Dire Straits. With more than $20 million in sales, it helped establish the whole CD business.

IT'S THE PITS

Sounds are stored on a CD as microscopic depressions, or pits, in its shiny aluminum-based layer. A pulsing laser beam aimed at the surface is reflected by a flat area between pits, creating a digital code of 1, or "on." A pit scatters the beam, so its reflection is not sensed, for a code of 0, or "off." The pits are arranged in a spiral path, like a record's grooves. With more than three billion pits, the whole path is 3 miles (5 kilometers) long.

15

Spinning CD

Flat areas between pits reflect laser beam (red).

Prism bends laser beam so it hits CD.

Lens

Laser

Laser beam bounces off flat areas on CD and is deflected by prism to encoder.

Signals are sent to amplifier.

CD players quickly became carry-anywhere personal stereos and moved from homes into cars. Because of the drawback that CD players could not record, as tape players could, many people ran the two systems side by side.

PC PARADE

The first desktop personal computers (PCs) appeared in the mid-1970s. Designed, in part, for computer enthusiasts, some were even available in kit form! In 1981, when corporate giant IBM introduced its PC, the march of computers into business, the media, and daily life began.

A NOVEL IDEA

Computers are as helpful as the programs, applications, and information fed into them. Around 1980, most people who had computer experience got it from work, using shared, sometimes room-size machines. The idea of a computer on your desk, available at any time, either at work or at home, to use as you chose, was a great novelty. Yet programs were limited, and, compared to modern versions, graphics and games were almost stone-aged.

Toshiba's 1987 laptop offered powerful computing to workers on the road or away from the office.

ADAPTABLE MACHINES

Despite their limitations, computers were popular because they were adaptable and flexible. The same machine could be used for accounting, writing, communication, and design — plus the occasional game! In the media, computers quickly had an impact on the timing-driven newspaper business. Using a desktop publishing program, one person could, in minutes, type the words, put in the pictures, and design the page on-screen, tasks that previously took several people several hours.

In 1983, when early portables were launched, some people believed that computers would always be only toys for the rich.

Word processor computers were ideal for fast communication. Their files were in electronic form, ready to be sent through a telecommunication network.

NEW PUBLICATIONS

The new ease of publishing encouraged some computer users to start low-budget newsletters or periodicals called "zines," such as a "fanzine" devoted to a particular music, movie, or sports star. Also, big companies started to send words and pictures between computers in their offices, via a telecommunication network. This kind of computer activity was the beginning of electronic mail, or e-mail.

By 1990, the offices of many businesses, especially media businesses such as this call center for the Sky media group, were dominated by computer screens, instead of typewriters and designers' drawing boards.

MOVING WITH THE TIMES

With computer efficiency finding its way into offices and industries, workers with old technology feared losing their jobs. In 1986 and 1987, London saw violent clashes as Fleet Street, the traditional newspaper and printing region, declined in power. Newspapers such as Eddy Shah's *Today*, the United Kingdom's first full-color daily, were produced using fewer people and more computers.

Eddy Shah started Today *in 1986.*

By the late 1980s, CDs were becoming the preferred format for multimedia computer programs combining images, graphics, music, sound effects, animation, and user interaction.

GOING MOBILE

In the early 1950s, the newly-invented transistor allowed electrical media gadgets, such as radios, TVs, and record players, to shrink significantly. The next big leap came in the early 1970s with Intel's first large-scale integrated circuits, or "chips."

Personal stereos became common in the early 1980s. They helped the popularity of radio and, through sales of both prerecorded and blank audiocassette tapes, also gave the music industry a boost.

EVEN SMALLER

Integrated circuits are made on slices of a semiconductor substance such as silicon. All of the electronic components, including thousands of transistors, resistors, and capacitors, are already connected, or integrated, into one giant, complex circuit that is microscopic in size. With the introduction of microchips, electronics entered another new age. Equipment became even smaller, lighter, and less power-hungry, so that batteries could supply enough electricity. Intel's microchips opened the way for personal, portable media gadgets.

The Sony that broke the sound barrier.

Until Sony introduced the Walkman (a stereo cassette player about the size of a cassette), there was no way to hear quality sound reproduction this good unless you bought a ticket to Carnegie Hall or sat home with an expensive component stereo.

Unfortunately, it was impossible to ski, jog, roller-skate or take a walk in a concert hall or your living room.

This is why on November 1, 1979, the Walkman took a historic step forward by combining incredible sound with total portability. What followed can only be described as a Sonic Boom.

Now people everywhere are taking their music with them, even if they're going nowhere fast. THE WALKMAN

SONY
THE ONE AND ONLY

Despite the fact that they could not record, the first 30,000 Sony Walkmans sold out in two months. The gadget quickly became a fashion item. Production of versions that could record started in 1982.

WALK, DON'T WALK

Transistor radios had been pocket-size since the 1950s. Small cassette tapes had been available since the 1960s. In 1979, Sony's Walkman combined the two, along with small earphones, for private, on-the-go listening of either recorded music or live radio broadcasts. A few years later, the CD version, Discman, appeared. Audio media now went anywhere people did.

TALK, DON'T TALK

Shrinking electronics was affecting many aspects of daily life, from televisions to washing machines. For decades, the outward appearance of telephones had changed very little. They were tabletop units with wires connected to a wall. When microchips allowed for radio transmitter-receivers small enough to fit into a handheld unit, telephones lost their wires. The world and its media were going "mobile."

Early handheld and in-car mobile phones developed from walkie-talkie technology used by emergency services and the military. By today's standards for size, they were giants!

IC "chip" in casing

Connectors to IC

Legs plug into main board.

CLEVER CHIPS

Integrated circuit (IC) technology raced forward during the 1970s and 1980s, packing millions of components onto a thin slice, or "chip," of silicon that was only a few square millimeters in size. The Central Processing Unit (CPU), or "main brain," of a computer doubled in speed and handling capacity approximately every eighteen months.

Some recording studios switched to magnetic digital audio tape (DAT), but DAT for home use lost out to CDs. DAT could record, but it could not skip almost instantly to any part of the music.

MUSIC REVOLUTION

As each generation of young people strives to be different from the generation before, new styles of music appear. The generations of the 1970s and 1980s were no exception. As soon as one new style became recognized and popular, another new style was needed.

Marc Bolan, the United Kingdom's "Bopping Elf," led the early 1970s glam rock band T. Rex.

In a flurry of swearing, spitting, and loud, fast music, punk rock pioneers the Sex Pistols burst onto the music scene in 1976. They outraged parents, the authorities, the establishment, and even music-lovers.

GLAM, DISCO, AND PUNK

In the early 1970s, the glamorous, or "glam," rock of David Bowie, Marc Bolan, and Kiss showed how sparkly costumes and spectacular stage shows could be as popular as the music itself. In 1977, the movie *Saturday Night Fever* launched actor John Travolta to stardom. The movie's Bee Gees sound track helped establish the flouncy soul- and funk-based style known as "disco." For those fed up with the glitter, punk rock went back to basics with its simple, aggressive, guitar-based sound.

CHANGE AND CHANGE AGAIN

In the 1980s, musical styles changed again. Grandmaster Flash and Melle Mel's *The Message* (1982) brought rap and hip-hop styles, which had developed in the United States, to a worldwide audience. The synthesizer sounds of microchip technology and a baggy-trousered "pirate" image signified the "new romantic" style of the groups Duran Duran, Spandau Ballet, Japan, and Visage.

MUSIC VIDEOS

In the midst of all these new styles, mainstream rock was still in safe hands as 1960s successes, such as the Rolling Stones, Pink Floyd, and Fleetwood Mac, joined by the Eagles and Abba, continued their colossal tours for older audiences. The rise of television channels that specialized in modern music, especially MTV, led to the production of promotional, or "promo," videos that could be shown on music shows, instead of having artists perform live. With the addition of lavish costumes and elaborate sets, music videos quickly became an art form.

Madonna was one of several singing-dancing-composing superstars to become established in the 1980s. Like a Virgin (1984) was her first global-hit album.

MUSIC EVERYWHERE

By the end of the 1980s, music, either recorded or on a radio, was almost everywhere. Kitchens, bedrooms, cars, pockets, belts, bicycles, skateboards, and school desks all were homes to various types of music equipment. More than 200 million CDs were being sold each year, far exceeding sales of, now old-fashioned, vinyl records.

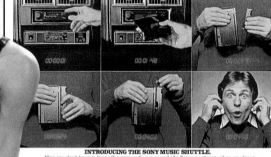

IT GOES FROM CAR STEREO TO PORTABLE IN 4.5 SECONDS.

INTRODUCING THE SONY MUSIC SHUTTLE.

Now you don't have to leave the extraordinary sound of a Sony car stereo when you leave your car. Instead, you can carry it with you, thanks to the Sony Music Shuttle. The first car stereo that turns into a portable stereo.

At the push of a button, the Music Shuttle's cassette player ejects, and is ready for a battery pack and headphones.

What's left behind in your dashboard is the Music Shuttle's AM/FM radio. A radio that delivers high-fidelity stereo even when the cassette player isn't in your car.

Also left behind is a large, conspicuous hole where the cassette player once was. A hole that will do more to discourage a thief than any alarm or lock.

All of which makes the Music Shuttle the first car stereo that, literally, leaves nothing to be desired.

SONY
THE ONE AND ONLY

A combination in-car to portable player

Music videos peaked with Michael Jackson's Thriller *(1983), from his 1982 album of the same name. This 14-minute video cost $8 million to make, more than many full-length movies of the time.*

BIG-MONEY MOVIES

At the movies, one 1970s film took in more money at the box office than any other movie that decade. This monster hit had a very memorable, often imitated, sound track — and a ferocious star!

OF SPIELBERG AND SPACE

The monster hit was *Jaws* (1975), and its director, Steven Spielberg (*b.* 1946), continued to dominate the film world of the 1970s and 1980s with more monster hits, including *Close Encounters of the Third Kind* (1977), *Raiders of the Lost Ark* (1981), and *E.T. The Extra-Terrestrial* (1982). Space became a major movie theme. Advanced special effects, complex robots, and computer animation accompanied young Luke Skywalker as he battled evil Darth Vader in *Star Wars* (1977), *The Empire Strikes Back* (1980), and *Return of the Jedi* (1983). A space crew struggled with a human-eating, acid-bleeding, stomach-exploding creature in *Alien* (1979). TV's *Star Trek* series generated feature-film spin-offs beginning in 1979.

22

Jaws *tapped into a basic human fear of deadly beasts from dark depths. The film included genuine suspense, and, compared to the "horror" movies released at that time, it had very little bad language or true violence.*

During the late 1980s, Steven Spielberg turned from deep-sea and deep-space fantasies to more serious, thoughtful subjects, directing films such as The Color Purple *(1985) and* Empire of the Sun *(1987). Despite their huge audiences, these movies were virtually ignored by the Hollywood-based awards organizations.*

An early multiplex in London, England

MOVIE THEATERS FIGHT BACK

Competing with television, home videos, and other domestic entertainment, such as computer games, movie theaters faced an uphill battle for audiences. In Britain, the number of moviegoers per year had peaked in 1946 at 1,650 million. By 1984, the number had plummeted to 55 million. Theaters responded by building complexes with five or more screens. These "multiplexes" offered a choice of movies and greater comfort, as well as more refreshments and movie merchandise. In 1985, the year multiplexes first opened, audience numbers began to climb.

REAL-LIFE THRILLERS

Major movie studios in the United States, which had been relatively quiet in the 1960s, came back with big-budget blockbusters in the 1970s. *The Godfather* (1972), a story of family life mixed with the murderous terror of organized crime, was the first film of a successful trilogy. *All The President's Men* (1976) and *The China Syndrome* (1979) dramatized real events — Watergate and the potential for meltdowns at nuclear power stations.

Using graphics and computers, Who Framed Roger Rabbit *(1988) combined cartoon animation with live action. Viewers were amazed at the seamless way the animated Roger interacted with live actor Bob Hoskins.*

In 1974, U.S. president Richard Nixon resigned over the Watergate scandal. All The President's Men *(1976) showed how journalists helped reveal Nixon's involvement in this break-in at the offices of rival politicians.*

DOWN UNDER

Outside the United States, several nations developed thriving movie industries, often with the help of government grants. Successful Australian films included *The Chant of Jimmie Blacksmith* (1978) and the first of the *Mad Max* series (1979), but Australian stars, such as Mel Gibson, soon relocated to Hollywood.

ART-TECHNO

During the 1980s, computer technology found its way into visual media such as printing, graphic design, and photography. Applications could manipulate shapes and colors with novel results, yet traditional art techniques continued to flourish.

SIMPLE YET ELEGANT

England's David Hockney (b. 1937) rose to prominence in the "pop art" movement of the 1960s. In the 1970s and 1980s, he continued to combine clean lines and bright colors with precise detail, elegant composition, and humor, creating art that reflected brash modern culture and advertising. In the mid-1970s, he also moved into set design for movies and theater productions.

24

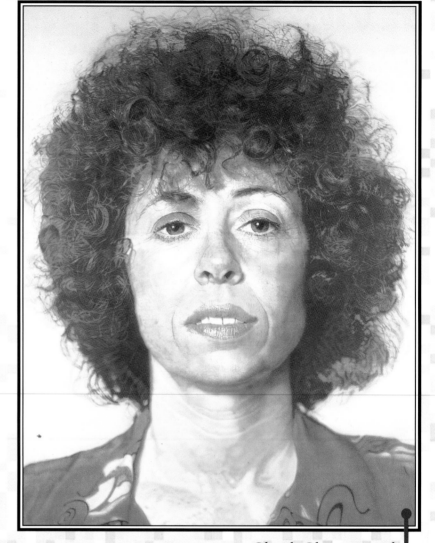

Chuck Close created huge, detailed, realistic paintings of photographs, usually faces. Linda (1976) is almost 10 feet (3 meters) tall. Close created other works in pencil and made mosaic-like pieces built up from fingerprints or blobs of paper.

British artist David Hockney worked with paints, photographs, silk screens, and other artistic media to design the set for Stravinsky's opera The Rake's Progress (1975).

MULTIMEDIA "PERFORMANCE ART"

Texas-born Robert Rauschenberg (*b.* 1925) continued his 1960s work with images from popular culture, which are included in his best-selling book *Rauschenberg Photographs* (1981). He experimented by combining photography with techniques such as silk-screening, synthesized sound, and theater, creating the medium of "performance art." Another U.S. artist, Chuck Close (*b.* 1940), developed photo-realism, making huge, detailed paintings from color photographs.

In 1987, Keith Haring (1958–1990) painted the mural Crack Is Wack *in New York City. Crack cocaine, a highly addictive drug, was a growing problem during the 1980s. The message of Haring's wall painting was that taking drugs (crack) was bad (wack).*

ELECTRONIC ARTIST?

The computer was a very flexible art tool — an electronic paintbrush. The way it worked led to exciting new techniques that could be done on-screen in seconds, making experimenting much easier and faster. In the late 1970s, some people suggested that a computer program could even learn to paint and, so, could become a famous artist in its own right.

Computers greatly expanded the variety of visual effects. A conventional image, such as Leonardo da Vinci's Mona Lisa, *could be pixilated, or turned into mosaic-like blocks of uniform colors.*

MASTER OF GRAPHIC DESIGN

One of the world's great graphic designers, New York-born Milton Glaser (*b.* 1929) has won every award in his field. His 1970s' book *Milton Glaser Graphic Design* is a classic. Glaser's works include posters, magazines, newspapers, record jackets, company logos, typefaces, and even building interiors. In 1987, he designed the symbol and the poster for the World Health Organization's international AIDS awareness campaign.

Glaser's use of the heart symbol for the word "love" has become the most frequently imitated piece of graphic design in human history.

MEDIA EMPIRES

The bosses of media empires have enormous power. Wealth, by itself, exerts great influence, but add media's mass communication to it, and a person can easily promote his or her own views, opinions, businesses, and ambitions.

NEW-AGE PRESS BARONS

The original media bosses were "press barons" who owned large newspapers and other print publication businesses. As the types of media grew to include radio, television, satellite, cable, music, and movies, the opportunities for multimedia empires also increased. Then, reports on a news channel could be carefully selected to favor the channel's owners, or a print publication could carry favorable publicity for another medium, such as a TV channel, in the same empire.

Cincinnati-born Ted Turner (b. 1938) built an Atlanta TV station into the huge WTBS cable-satellite network, founded CNN, owned sports teams, and is a keen yachtsman and an environmentalist as well.

Czech-born Robert Maxwell (1923–1991) built a British publishing empire that included Pergamon Press, the Mirror newspapers, and Macmillan Publishers. Maxwell died suspiciously, leaving behind massive fraud and debt.

26

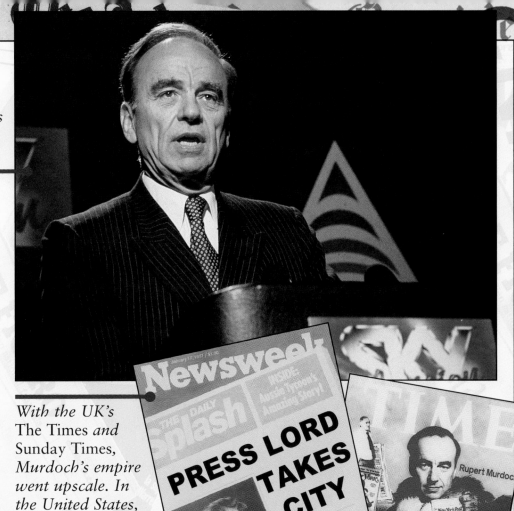

Australian Rupert Murdoch (b. 1931) started his country's first national daily newspaper, The Australian, *in 1964. He also took over tabloids, such as Britain's* The Sun *and* The New York Post, *and controlled numerous magazines.*

NEW CHALLENGERS

In the 1980s, TV, in particular, changed rapidly, with stations, channels, and shows frequently being bought and sold. The big U.S. commercial networks, ABC, CBS, and NBC, were challenged by newer groups, such as Fox. By 1990, the Fox network had seven stations, more than 120 associated companies, and links with newspapers and many other kinds of media.

TOO MUCH POWER?

In Britain, the commercial Direct Broadcast Satellite (DBS) groups, Sky and British Satellite Broadcasting (BSB), challenged the BBC and ITV network duo. Similar events were occurring in other countries, too. One empire's radio, television, publishing, and other media joined forces to promote each other over their competitors. Worries grew that too much power was held by too few people and was being used unfairly to obtain special favors in business and politics and to influence voters in elections.

With the UK's The Times *and* Sunday Times, *Murdoch's empire went upscale. In the United States, he purchased 20th Century Fox films and Fox TV. He also bought European Sky/BSB satellite TV. Murdoch became a U.S. citizen in 1985.*

27

Silvio Berlusconi (b. 1936)

SILVIO

In 1980, property developer Silvio Berlusconi founded Italy's first national commercial TV network, Canale 5. More TV stations followed, along with Publitalia 80 advertising, the huge Panorama-Mondadori publishing group, department stores, and large investments in Italian movies. In the late 1980s, Berlusconi took control of the AC Milan soccer club and aired plans to use his media to fulfill his political goal of becoming Italian prime minister, which he did in 1994 and again in 2001.

WRONGS AND RIGHTS

The media, especially TV, radio, newspapers, and other means of communicating news, can be tremendous forces for good. Investigative reporters, for example, regularly expose crimes, cover-ups, corruption, and injustice. The news media can also be powerful allies to campaigns fighting for a cause.

28

SOUTH AFRICA'S ECONOMIC TREMORS
THE INTERNATIONAL NEWSMAGAZINE
Newsweek
September 9, 1985
WHITEWASH?
France's Greenpeace Report
NUCLEAR FREE PACIFIC

MEXICO'S EARTHQUAKE TRAGEDY
Making Cities Safer
Newsweek
September 30, 1985
THE INTERNATIONAL NEWSMAGAZINE
GREENPEACE
FIASCO
François Mitterrand
And Charles Hernu
Number 39

SCHEME BACKFIRES

Environmental groups such as Greenpeace make skillful use of the media to publicize their causes. In 1985, explosions sank the Greenpeace ship *Rainbow Warrior* in New Zealand's Auckland harbor, where it was preparing to take action against nuclear detonations by France in the Pacific. Evidence soon came to light that the French government might have been involved in the sinking. This news led to fierce criticism of France, which included some allegations of state-sponsored terrorism, and gave Greenpeace a great deal of publicity.

Although Greenpeace lost a ship, it gained tremendous sympathy and publicity after reports that French agents might have sabotaged its antinuclear protest.

In 1987, Greenpeace took direct action in a protest against burning toxic waste and dumping it at sea. With daring stunts, Greenpeace used the news media to reach millions of people.

BAN THE BURN
GREENPEACE

GROWING GREEN

Oil shortages and price increases during the 1960s had led to long lines at gas pumps in 1973. The oil crisis created a new awareness of energy use and conservation as part of a blossoming "green movement." Most of the media played a part by reporting the news and enabling commentators and experts to explain the problems and present environmentally friendly solutions.

The fall of Germany's Berlin Wall signaled an end to the Cold War between the USSR and the USA and that stand-off's nuclear threats. In 1991, the communist-based Soviet Union began breaking up into separate countries.

MEDIA FREEDOM

In most democratic nations, the media are free to report facts and opinions as long as they do not infringe on basic laws, such as libel or obscenity. Wartime is different. Giving out details of attack plans or the locations of planes and ships could cost lives and help the enemy. In 1982, Argentina invaded British territories of the Falkland Islands, in the South Atlantic. During the conflict that followed, government, armed forces, and media worked closely together to present the news as completely and accurately as possible — but not too openly.

During the conflict in the Falkland Islands, the British media were carefully monitored by authorities.

BIG TROUBLES

Bad news, however, continued. Acid rain, a thinning ozone layer, and possible early signs of global warming made big headlines in the 1980s. In 1986, a nuclear power station at Chernobyl, in the Ukraine, exploded, causing a mammoth ecological disaster. Another followed in 1989, as the super-tanker *Exxon Valdez* spilled a massive oil slick off the coast of Alaska. Despite the many rights, would wrongs continue to dominate into the 1990s?

In 1984, the HIV virus was identified, and Acquired Immune Deficiency Syndrome (AIDS) became a recognized condition. Media campaigns alerted people to the risks.

Virus, magnified 135,000 times, destroying T cell

· TIME LINE ·

	WORLD EVENTS	HEADLINES	MEDIA EVENTS	TECHNOLOGY	THE ARTS
1970	•U.S. troops sent into Cambodia	•Students shot at Ohio's Kent State University	•George C. Scott refuses Academy Award for Patton	•Corning Glass develops optical fiber	•John Updike: Rabbit Redux
1971	•Uganda: Amin in power •Greenpeace founded	•Nixon lifts 20-year U.S. trade embargo with China	•Newspapers switch from letterpress to offset	•First word processor (Wang 1200)	•Stanley Kubrick: A Clockwork Orange
1972	•Direct rule in Ulster •U.S. troops leave Vietnam	•SALT (Strategic Arms Limitation Treaty) signed	•"Pentagon Papers" are published in NY Times	•First video games played through a TV set	•Alan Alda stars in M*A*S*H TV series
1973	•Yom Kippur War •OPEC raises oil prices	•First U.S. space station, Skylab, launched	•People magazine begins •Sydney Opera House opens	•Xerox develops Ethernet computer network	•Pink Floyd: Dark Side of the Moon
1974	•Turkey invades Cyprus and occupies one-third	•Nixon resigns due to Watergate scandal	•The BBC offers teletext service	•First solid-state video cameras	•Stephen King: Carrie •James Michener: Centennial
1975	•Cambodia overrun by Pol Pot's Khmer Rouge	•Vietnam War ends	•Jaws is first film to earn over $100 million	•BASIC programming language for PCs	•Queen: "Bohemian Rhapsody"
1976	•China: Chairman Mao dies	•Student protests in Soweto start deadly riots	•U.S.'s Viking space probe sends pictures from Mars	•Fiber-optic cables first used for telecommunication	•Peter Finch and Faye Dunaway star in Network
1977	•South Africa: Steven Biko dies in custody	•Elvis Presley dies	•Atari and Nintendo computer games go on sale	•Dolby noise reduction system introduced	•Woody Allen: Annie Hall •George Lucas: Star Wars
1978	•Egypt and Israel sign Camp David treaty	•New pope, John Paul II, elected	•London's The Times is out of print for 11 months	•First laser disc systems for home movies	•Hockney designs set for opera The Magic Flute
1979	•Iran: Khomeini in power •USSR invades Afghanistan	•Thatcher is Britain's first woman prime minister	•Alien movie prompts UFO abduction claims	•Sony introduces Walkman personal stereo	•Francis Ford Coppola: Apocalypse Now
1980	•Start of Iran-Iraq War •Poland: Solidarity	•John Lennon murdered in New York City	•Ted Turner launches CNN 24-hour cable TV	•Sony camcorder •France: Minitel telephone	•Norman Mailer: Executioner's Song
1981	•U.S.: Reagan wounded in assassination attempt	•Prince Charles of England marries Diana Spencer	•Music video channel MTV begins on cable TV	•Laptop computers introduced	•Terry Gilliam: Time Bandits
1982	•Falklands War; Britain defeats Argentina	•Princess Grace of Monaco dies	•Michael Jackson's Thriller album sells 25 million copies	•Audio compact disc (CD) introduced	•Ridley Scott: Blade Runner •Steven Spielberg: E.T.
1983	•U.S. and Caribbean troops invade Grenada	•Poland's Lech Walesa wins Nobel Peace Prize	•U.S.: First episode of nighttime soap Dynasty	•First microcomputer with graphical user interface	•The Eurythmics: "Sweet Dreams"
1984	•India: leader Indira Gandhi assassinated	•Famine devastates Ethiopia	•Robert Maxwell buys Mirror Group Newspapers	•Sony introduces Discman	•Tom Clancy: The Hunt for Red October
1985	•Italian cruise ship Achille Lauro hijacked	•Auckland explosions sink Greenpeace ship	•AOL begins as Quantum Computer Services	•Television broadcasts in stereo	•Sting: The Dream of the Blue Turtles
1986	•USSR: Chernobyl nuclear disaster	•U.S. space shuttle Challenger explodes	•U.S. television adds Fox network	•Laser printers replace dot matrix	•Paul Hogan stars in Crocodile Dundee
1987	•Black Monday stock market crash	•British envoy Terry Waite is hostage in Beirut	•U.S. government deregulates cable	•Digital audio tape (DAT) introduced	•Tom Wolfe: Bonfire of the Vanities
1988	•End of Iran-Iraq war	•Pan Am jet explodes over Lockerbie, Scotland	•Rushdie's The Satanic Verses angers Muslims	•Prodigy offers dial-up Internet service	•Jeff Koons: Popples •Van Halen: OU812
1989	•China: Tiananmen Square massacre	•Fall of Berlin Wall unites East and West Germany	•Last London newspapers produced on Fleet Street	•Japan broadcasts analog HDTV programs	•Keith Haring: Ignorance=Fear

GLOSSARY

airtime: any time during which a radio or television station is actively broadcasting.

analog: related to a form of electronic transmission, as in a conventional radio or telephone, that adds signals of varying frequency or amplitude (height) to waves of alternating electromagnetic current.

applications: computer software, such as word processing or a spreadsheet, that is programmed to perform particular tasks.

cable TV: a broadcasting system in which television signals picked up by a main antenna are distributed by means of fiber-optic cables to the receiver sets of paid subscribers.

DBS (Direct Broadcast Satellite): a broadcasting system in which TV signals are transmitted by satellite directly to the receiver dishes of individual users, rather than to the dishes of TV networks.

digital: related to an electronic system that uses numbers, or digits, usually 0 and 1, to form codes that represent information, or data.

photo-realism: a style of painting that represents subjects in precise and accurate detail.

semiconductor: a solid substance with an ability to conduct electricity that, at high temperatures, is almost as great as a metal and, at low temperatures, is almost nonexistent, making it a good medium for controlling electrical current.

teletext: a broadcasting system that transmits text and graphics over unused portions of TV signals and displays them on receivers that are equipped with a decoder.

time-shift devices: electronic equipment designed to record network television broadcasts for viewing at a later time.

MORE BOOKS TO READ

1970s: Turbulent Times. 20th Century Music (series). Malcolm Hayes (Gareth Stevens)

1980s: From Ronald Reagan to MTV. Decades of the 20th Century (series). Stephen Feinstein (Raintree/Steck-Vaughn)

Beyond the Rainbow Warrior. Michael Morpurgo, editor (Pavilion Books)

Chuck Close Up Close. Jan Greenberg and Sandra Jordan (Dorling Kindersley)

Desktop Publishing: The Art of Communication. Media Workshop (series). John Madama (Lerner)

A Look at Life in the Seventies. R. G. Grant (Raintree/Steck-Vaughn)

Movie Science: 40 Mind-Expanding, Reality-Bending, Starstruck Activities for Kids. Jim Wiese (Wiley)

Music CDs: From Start to Finish. Made in the USA (series). Mindi Rose Englart (Blackbirch)

Ted Turner: Television's Triumphant Tiger. Wizards of Business (series). Rebecca Stefoff (Garrett Educational)

The World of Computers and Communication. An Inside Look (series). Ian Graham (Gareth Stevens)

WEB SITES

Computer History Museum: Timeline of Computer History. *www.computerhistory.org/timeline/*

Haring Kids. *www.haringkids.com*

How Stuff Works: Electronics! *www.howstuffworks.com/category.htm?cat=Elec*

Live Aid: July 13th; 1985. *touslescochonssontronds. chez.tiscali.fr/dazibao/liveaid/*

Due to the dynamic nature of the Internet, some web sites stay current longer than others. To find additional web sites, use a reliable search engine with one or more of the following keywords: *Berlin Wall, Chernobyl, compact disc, disco, fiber optics, glam rock, Greenpeace, Intel, microchip, Rupert Murdoch, satellite television,* and *VCR.*

INDEX